inspired? get writing!

inspired?
get writing!

Further new poems and short stories
inspired by the collection of the
National Galleries of Scotland

National Galleries of Scotland

*in association with the Scottish Poetry Library
and the English-Speaking Union Scotland*

A NOTE ON THE CATEGORIES

The entries are accompanied by a note indicating into which category they were entered:

CATEGORY A   under 12 years

CATEGORY B   12 – 15 years (2011: 12–14 years)

CATEGORY C   16 – 18 years (2011: 15–18 years)

CATEGORY D   unpublished adults

CATEGORY E   published adults

Published by the Trustees of the
National Galleries of Scotland 2011

ISBN 978 1 906270 42 1

Designed by Dalrymple
Typeset in Verdigris and Modern no.20
Printed on Hello Matt 150gsm by Nicholson & Bass

National Galleries of Scotland is a charity registered
in Scotland no.SC003728

www.nationalgalleries.org

NATIONAL
GALLERIES
SCOTLAND

'The three of us went to see the painter in her studio – a big white room except where she'd spilled paint. Which was most places including her clothes. We told her that our wee baby brother was being born and that we were to help name it. She asked how we knew it was a boy and we told her that granny tested mam's belly with a wedding ring.

'How absolutely wonderful,' the painter said and went away and came back with a name book for us to look at while we waited for the baby. She said that I must bring the baby and she might paint it. I told her I would have to see and she laughed. I saw one of her paintings once – one of some children. The baby better not look like that.'

from *Street Kids* by Philip Murnin

Foreword

The art of marrying words and pictures is not new. Some of our best-loved poems and stories have sprung from great works of art, and many artists have been inspired by great literature. Yet it seemed very exciting and innovative six years ago, when the *inspired? get writing!* competition was first launched, to ask people to produce writing based on the collection of the National Galleries of Scotland. The partner organisations – the National Galleries of Scotland, the English-Speaking Union Scotland and, from the second year onwards, the Scottish Poetry Library – all hoped that this would encourage a new generation of writers to seek inspiration from art.

The response has been all that we could have wished for, and more. Over the past six years we have received almost 5,000 poems and stories, from individuals and schools all over Scotland and Britain, and as far away as the deserts of Afghanistan and the plains of Mongolia. Thanks to the internet, our national collection has become accessible, and thereby truly international, through the National Galleries' website. So for schools, with the collection at their fingertips, the competition offers teachers and pupils an exciting creative template and the kind of cross-curricular exploration and experience which is at the heart of the Scottish Curriculum for Excellence. Each year, new writers of all ages take their inspiration from online images, as well as well-thumbed books, tucked-away postcards, and of course, the original works on display across the Galleries. Their entries are fresh and exciting, moving and humorous.

We have been very fortunate in receiving sponsorship for this competition from the Gordon Fraser Charitable Trust, which has enabled us to produce accompanying anthologies. We are sure that this third volume, featuring the winning entries from 2010 and 2011, and the work of almost thirty previously unpublished writers, will delight readers as much as the previous two. It may be going too far to second Lewis Carroll's Alice, herself memorably illustrated by John Tenniel, who asked 'What is the use of a book without pictures?' But you will see in these pages that the writing offers a new interpretation of the art, which in turn seems to offer almost limitless inspiration.

This competition would not be possible without the help and support of many people and institutions. The *Scotsman* has supported the competition from the start, which has proved invaluable, and we are extremely grateful to our judges who give up so much of their time to assist us. We are also very grateful to the teachers and parents who support the competition, and hope this encourages a lifelong love of writing for the younger entrants. We warmly thank the competition organisers, Linda McClelland (National Galleries of Scotland), Lorna Irvine (Scottish Poetry Library), and Suzanne Ensom (English-Speaking Union Scotland) who work so hard to make this competition a success.

Most of all, we thank and celebrate the writers who have put pen to paper, fingers to keys, and sent in their entries. We hope you enjoy them as much as we have, and if you are feeling inspired, next year … get writing!

JOHN LEIGHTON
Director-General, National Galleries of Scotland

JON DYE
Chairman, English-Speaking Union Scotland

ROBYN MARSACK
Director, Scottish Poetry Library

NATIONAL GALLERIES SCOTLAND

English-Speaking Union

SCOTTISH POETRY LIBRARY
By leaves we live

Gordon Fraser Charitable Trust

That Little Unquenchable Spark

Susan Mansfield

Where do you get your ideas from? Writers quickly weary of the question. One can begin to understand Neil Gaiman's habitual response: 'From a little ideas shop in Bognor Regis'. Or Philip Pullman, who once told a questioner that he subscribed online to Ideas'R'Us. Without batting an eyelid, the person asked for the web address.

The word 'inspiration', with its overtones of gods and muses, has fallen out of fashion. But readers and writers alike recognise that there is an element in the writing process which is mysterious: the moment of illumination which seizes the attention, the little unquenchable spark which unleashes the imagination. This process cannot be fully understood, nor will it respond to our demands. And because writers know that it arrives without invitation and can depart just as suddenly, they have their own superstitions. Keats liked to put on a clean shirt. Andrew Motion writes in pencil in a particular type of notebook. Singer-songwriter Beth Orton might put on her big pink hat. The muse is fickle, and each has their own way of humouring her.

inspired? get writing?, the creative writing competition run by the National Galleries of Scotland in partnership with the English-Speaking Union Scotland and the Scottish Poetry Library, began with a very simple idea: that a great collection of art is a repository of inspiration. With a collection as extensive and wide-ranging as that of the National Galleries of Scotland, who could fail to find something to inspire them? If proof of cross fertilisation between art and writing were needed, it came almost immediately. As entries flooded in from both children and adults, there could be no doubt that seeing a work of art could spark a writer's creativity, offer a fresh perspective, suggest a new way to tackle a subject. This book, which publishes the winning entries from two years of the competition alongside the work of art which inspired each, allows us to observe up close some of the ways in which this works.

First, there are paintings which seem to invite stories. Monet's *Shipping by Moonlight* is full of intrigue and danger, sparking tales of storms and pirates. Writers young and old have been drawn to Joan Eardley's portraits of Glasgow street children, each of whom seems to have their own story to tell. More than one writer has been unable to resist a painting like El Greco's *Fábula*, with its implied narrative of darkness and secrets.

Other works do the opposite: they keep their stories close to their chests. Yet, every year as judges we are surprised by the way in which abstract, elusive works of art inspire good writing. Jessica Mustard (under 12s) found the story of a whole family in the abstract shapes of Lyubov Popova's *Painterly Architectonic*; Sarah Mcilwham (12–14s) wrote a sustained and often amusing essay on the difficulty of clearing one's head after seeing Man Ray's *Aviary (La Volière)*; and Joseph Reed (unpublished adults) gives us a fresh take on jealousy in *Paint*, inspired by William Johnstone's white-on-white abstract, *Embryonic*.

Sometimes writers imagine themselves into the world of the artist, getting under the skin of the creative process. Jamie Arnaud (under 12s) has written a witty and descriptive poem based on an ink sketch by James Guthrie, all the more remarkable for being full of colours when the sketch has none. James Gao (15–18s), inspired by one of Turner's Venice watercolours, addresses the subject of slippage between the moment as it is lived, the memory and the painting. Laura Helyer (unpublished adults), writing about Joan Eardley's field landscape, looks at how the artist strives physically to capture that moment: 'See how the paint soaks down into the act of remembrance…'

Writers are like magpies. We collect things that sparkle: phrases, people, places, memories. Sometimes the function of inspiration is to forge a connection, shed light on something particular in the memory banks and draw it out into a new context. Pisanello's *Study of a Young Man with his Hands Tied behind his Back* was enough to prompt Keir Ogilvy (under 12s) to write a searing account of what it is like to be a slave. John Bellany's *Allegory* so lends itself to Heather Reid's (published adults) dark futuristic tale of poisoned seas that it seems almost to have been painted for that purpose. Wendy McMurdo's photograph *Girl with Bears, Royal Museum of Scotland, Edinburgh*, prompted Annie Forbes (12–15s) to write vividly from the perspective of both the child and the bear.

Even when the writer touches lightly on the work of art before taking flight on their own journey, there is still a sense in which the painting plays a crucial role. Guinevere Glasfurd-Brown (published adults) takes Julian Opie's *Imagine You are Driving 1* and around it creates a fragile moment of bonding between a young asylum seeker and his detention officer over a driving game at a motorway service station. Damien Hirst's spin painting *Beautiful C* inspired Josephine Brogan (published adults) to write a tender sonnet about the moon and motherhood. Iona Byrne (15–18s) writes on Robert Henderson Blythe's '*Existence Precarious*' but imagines not the battlefields of Flanders but a wife at home seeing her husband in her own imagination.

But all of this is only half the story. Less than half. It is one thing for an idea to be sparked, another to turn it into a finished piece of work. After the match has been struck, then comes the fanning into flame, the graft of writing and rewriting. Not for nothing did American writer Mary Heaton Vorse say: 'The art of writing is the art of applying the seat of the pants to the seat of the chair.' The writers in this book have done both things. They have paid attention to the spark of an idea and had faith in it, and they have worked with it, bringing to bear their own skills, time and toil. They have applied both inspiration and perspiration. Now they can enjoy the fruits of their labours in print. Hats off to them.

Joan Among Nets

by LAURA HELYER

The blue boat was our escape.
See how it ran and ran into the sleek, green sea.

We did not have to push, or spade the waves.
The foam, spray, the rush – zinc white,

the cottages tipping the cliff,
chops of boulder clay – red ochre,

vermilion fields of valved earth,
heavy slates of weather, a continent of cloud.

***

The slubbed nets haired the depths.
I wanted their slim, free bodies

hooked to a line of sun.
Flicker and twist, a meeting of eyes,

flicker, and then nothing.
Bottle-green, royal blue.

Deep, calmed silence.
Your breath; mine.

***

Tonight I will hold you again
stickered with fish scales,

sequin kisses I call them,
shining your skin, your hair

the flavour of old ocean and love,
sung on my tongue.

[CATEGORY D]

JOAN EARDLEY
Boats on the Shore, c.1963
GMA 1036 · Scott Hay Collection: presented 1967

Coloured by Mischief

by JAMIE ARNAUD

It dawns a perfect morning in Cockburnspath:
a sunless September sky of creamy porridge
poured on patchwork fields of nettle green and chaffinch brown.

A trusty umbrella deflects the glare of bleached clouds.
My dark suit and cap, like an upturned exclamation mark,
inkblots the autumn landscape.

I prepare my palette of stone-dyke greys and breadbasket browns,
half-watched by a Highland bull, thick-spread
in a coat of butter-soft cinnamon.

As time watches, fingertips of breeze ruffle the trees,
then a soft Scottish smir turns to stair rods.
Canvas, paints and easel are hastily strapped on my back.

Startled by this curious, canvas-armoured armadillo,
the bull stares me out, full of bramble-eyed irritation and contempt,
regarding me like a toro bravo his matador.

I stumble home, a wet-footed rivulet
trailing over muddy stone and stile
to a buttermilk farmhouse framed by robin-red rowans.

That evening, in copper-beech firelight, my mind drifts backwards.
An eccentric moment dances mischievously from memory to paper:
Fine weather for my 50 × 30!

[CATEGORY A]

SIR JAMES GUTHRIE
'Fine Weather for my 50 × 30'
D 5102.27 · Dr Camilla M. Uytman Gift 1981

Starfish Villanelle

by CALISTA WINSTANLEY

The storm had faded, leaving flotsam dry
And wood salt-bleached. Amidst it all they lay,
A beach of stars, the ocean's voiceless sigh.

Unnoticed by the weary passers-by;
Five legs flung out, like sunlight gone astray.
One last salute: farewell to sea and sky.

From the cold sea thrown onto sand to die
In their bright thousands, carpeting the bay.
A beach of stars, the ocean's voiceless sigh.

The sun, in horror, closed its blood-streaked eye,
Left beach and stars to merge into the grey.
One last salute: farewell to sea and sky.

For time must change, as tide ebbs low or high
And when their hour had come they could not stay.
A beach of stars, the ocean's voiceless sigh.

When sunset comes for us, what use to cry
Or mourn short days? Just close your eyes and say:
'One last salute: farewell to sea and sky.'

That day when stranded sunbeams still did lie,
To rot throughout the night and through the day,
A beach of stars, the ocean's voiceless sigh,
One last salute: farewell to sea and sky.

[CATEGORY C]

EILEEN AGAR
Fish Circus, 1939
GMA 3938 · Bequeathed by Gabrielle Keiller 1995

Girl from the Polders

by ANDY JACKSON

In her youth she worked and drank
and danced on artificial islands, lying low
on concrete piles, a gag in the throat
of a gulping estuary. Living with
the prospect of Atlantean collapse
into the shallows turned her on,
made each day a mortal dare. From then
she always lived on reclaimed ground,
on floating fens and marshes, or a year
on Black Sea salt-pans where the waters
turned to heavy air. She settled down
behind the dykes and tidal booms
of Europe, thrilled by threat of flood
each year as oceans stared her out.
She was deaf to claims that she'd be safe
on mountains or in landlocked fields.
She knew the plates were always shifting,
while she slept the continents made fire together.

Her men were all poor swimmers, in too deep,
rescued from maternal homes, some pulled
from sodden benches in the park, or met in rain
at prison gates. She gave them mouth-to-mouth
and wrang them out, taught them strokes she knew,
then led them out beyond the danger flags
to where she had dominion over tides.
She had faith in anything that she could build,
mistrusting the chicaneries of nature,
excited by the thought her men could leave
at any time, return to priggish mothers,
hit the welcome bottle, maybe kill again.

She knows enough of tides to turn her back
on them, embrace the shallow breathing
of the sea. She sits in darkness, in control,
monitoring rates of flow and regulating sluices,
lowering the barrage, holding back the flood.

[CATEGORY E]

CALUM COLVIN
Venus Anadyomene (after Titian), 1998
GMA 4292 · Presented by the artist 1999

The Long Night

by CATRIONA GELLATLY

The moon, only just visible
Through those darkening clouds,
The waves, slashing the sides of the ship
Chopping together like an angry shark's jaws.
Those strong wooden beams,
Steady in place,
Like the bones of a body,
The final piece without which
No puzzle is complete.
Thunder and lightning
Waiting to strike,
I knew then we were in for
A very long night.

Above the whirling winds
And the whipping waters,
The never failing sails fly.
And present,
The always steady wheel,
The comforting open map,
Never losing course.
Those moonlight beams
Reflect off the dark waters
Where who knows what may lurk.

The Frenchmen sing and swing
Blindly to and fro from the ropes,
The more cautious down below,
The effects of wine, oh what a show.
The opposing ships,
One on our tail and one in the distance,
The first a cargo ship,
With a nerve-wracking persistence.

The water still murky,
The clouds still dark,
The waves crashing against the rocks,
Bashing and bruising with all their knocks.
Thunder and lightning
Waiting to strike,
I knew then we were in for
A very long night.

[CATEGORY A]

18

CLAUDE MONET
A Seascape, Shipping by Moonlight, c.1864
NG 2399 · Purchased 1980

19

One Ale

by PHOEBE CREHAN

There's a man who keeps coming into the Stag Tavern (where I work) every night. He comes in his black coat and sits at the same table right next to the window and orders one ale. The first night he came it was rather busy and I came over to serve him.

'So what will it be then, sir?' I asked.

'One ale, please,' he replied and then took out some paper and started to sketch the view from the window.

Now a bit about me – my name is Rosie Burns. I'm twenty-one and my family own the Stag Tavern. It's right on Princes Street and you can look out of the windows up the street towards Calton Hill and Arthur's Seat. I used to help serve the drinks sometimes when I was little but I have been working here officially at the Stag now for three years, since 1822.

* * *

This is his sixth night in a row of coming in and having his one ale. It's a cold and very windy autumn day and it's been quite busy.

'I wonder where that man is: the one that orders one ale and draws in his book,' I say to Sophie the other waitress. But she's a bit preoccupied with a beer stain on her apron. (We have to wear them – they are bright red and usually have many stains on them.)

'I don't know,' replies Sophie. 'Maybe he's stopped coming. I didn't like him – coming in every night, doing the same thing. It's very strange.'

'I think it's quite interesting,' I say.

'Well, that's your opinion,' says Sophie. Then the door opens and in comes the man.

He sits at the same table as always and I walk over to him.

'One ale, sir?'

'Yes, please.'

I go over to the bar, where Sophie is pouring the ale into mugs.

'One ale, please,' I say to Sophie as she pours one mug after another.

'Do you think I should ask him what he's doing?' I ask her.

'Oh don't bother me now, Rosie! I'm busy,' Sophie says.

I walk over to him with the ale and place it on the table.

'Thank you.'

'If you don't mind me asking, sir, what are you doing?' I ask.

'Actually, I'm drawing a picture, and no, I don't mind you asking. After all, you have been serving me for three weeks now.'

'I'm Rosie – Rosie Burns.'

'Lovely to meet you Rosie. I'm Alexander Nasmyth.'

'So, what are you drawing, Mr Nasmyth?'

'I'm drawing Princes Street.'

'May I have a look?'

'Of course.'

He holds up his sketch – it's wonderful – just like the street outside the window, with all the people milling about.

'That's wonderful!' I exclaim.

'Thank you, Rosie.'

'Are you going to sell it?'

'No. Actually a gallery has decided to take it so that many people can see it.'

'Can I go and see the picture?'

'Yes, of course you can.'

* * *

I'm going to the gallery today to see the picture. It's very cold so I'm wearing my navy cloak. It's not far to the gallery. Some children are playing in a puddle and one of them splashes muddy water all down the front of my red apron.

'Sorry miss!' says the boy.

'It's alright,' I reply (although it isn't).

I walk into the ornate gallery. There are lots of very well-dressed ladies and gentlemen. I feel quite embarrassed because I'm just wearing a plain old cloak, dress and apron. After a while I find the picture that Mr Nasmyth drew, only now it's been coloured and it's beautiful!

Then I notice a small figure in the foreground wearing a red apron.

ALEXANDER NASMYTH
Princes Street with the Commencement of the Building of the Royal Institution, 1825
NG 2542 · Presented by Sir David Baird 1991

Misbegotten

by LEMUEL JONE

The Manor came down to a younger son
soon after his brothers were lost
in the mires of Passchendaele.
The 14th Earl cared nothing for the land,
and was easily relieved of it, with little art.
From his club in Limerick
he signed away a barren moor
for interment of the fief's unportioned dead –
only setting down engraving of a slate
for those forgotten long before they died.

Nearest a salted lowland waste
where stones gave way to bitter weeds,
raddled whores and rovers,
starveling crones,
excommunicants in rows,
the carrion of gallows and of jails
were lowered down,
spoken of, or not, and shovelled in.
Among them, too, an uncoffined girl,
priestcraft and hallowed earth denied,
gone underground as earthfill in a sack.

Coming out of early Mass,
fishwives whispered fearfully
of sin beyond redemption,
of one more suicide gone home to Hell.
Peat cutters resting on their spades,
Tinkers, shills and barrow boys,
Nuns with downcast eyes and busy beads –
all recalled a silent stray
with dark unsmiling eyes.
None had memories of a ruined child;
all forgot her in a day.

With hoar frost on the shingle and the tide well out,
the girl had often gleaned the longshore drift
for broken wood, and warmed herself
in the wreckage of the *Anne Marie*.
After a shop-soiled bun or a few discarded plums
she sat with feet to the flames, shawled in sacks,
and waited out the day.

A secret boy, too strange for home or town,
sheltered in a rotten barge and lived on razor clams.
She would see him on his belly,
moving with the falling tide,
salting burrows on his way.
Although she never asked and never would,
a few were sometimes wrapped in weed
and left outside her lair.
In Spring her thanks in plovers' eggs
were found among his treasures.

When limpets shone and curlews called
and stonecrop flowers lit the dunes,
two bathless children foraged up the strand.
Tide pool crabs and yellow minnows
filled a kettle found among the dross.
Then, sharing done, with no 'sleep well',
both hurried back to ground,
too lost in fear for trust to find a voice.

They gathered shoreline kale
that helped their bones,
samphire in the distant marsh,
and iron pots from just below the sand.
It was enough, until the Garda came.

Too wild by far, and wary, the boy was never found;
but she was down with fever in her bones.
Her whispered pleas were never heard,
too busy in their duties were the law.
The mother took her in because she must
and dumped her in the byre with the dogs.

Alone among the dying ships,
the boy awoke to hear his friend in pain.
Scrambling for candle ends
he ran too late to bring her to his care.

Beyond the darkened sand, among the rocks,
she howled at Heaven, cursed the living God,
and walked into the kind, obliging sea.
He found her in a shroud of bladderwrack,
rejected by the faithless deep,
the last to wrong her small exhausted soul.

They forced the mother to the shore
to give the child a name.
Sour to be wakened in the freezing dawn
she nodded, spat downwind,
pointed to the distant charnel ground,
and hurried back to her infectious bed.

The County field was nearly full, he saw,
they'd need another in a year or two.
The boy leaned down to touch the lettered stone
and laid another seashell on her grave.
With a Connemara wind blowing salt into his eyes,
he staked the land beside her for his own.
A passing digger, fearful of a curse,
swore an oath to Jude
that none would lie in his appointed ground.
Content, the gentle child remained a while,
not lonely now, and nevermore alone.

[CATEGORY D]

New mandates in the western towns
had reinforced the feeble childcare act.
Runaways and orphans,
the never sought or claimed,
were found and washed
and harried up the steps of home,
to make their peace and founder out of sight.

GERALD LESLIE BROCKHURST
Peasant Girl
GMA 4850 · Presented by Mr Richard Woodward 2005

Movement

by JAMES RODERICK BURNS

Begin with a bird –
a blackbird in flight, head cocked
towards hedgerows and streamers

of unruly smoke
rising up into the frame,
wings shying from unseen fires.

*

Remember the day?
Only the washing lifting
above the garden's green edge,

my fingers shielding
a fag from the snouting wind.
Everything else is stillness.

*

Under belling skirts
the pale valley multiplies
field over field, farm to farm

as each pair of eyes
holds its gaze, a horse startles
at the fork of a crossroads.

He asked, so I sat
stiffly on the art-room stool,
daylight pooling in my lap.

When it was finished
I had grown into the world,
my portrait spread like fingers.

*

We ride the smoke-trail
to a fat slice of sky, blue
only at its calm centre

where airy linens,
patience and expectation
jostle but will not be cowed.

*

That severe parting,
eyebrows lancing the heavens,
a great bloodred slash of mouth –

despite the dull paint
I outshone them all, quite shamed
the apples at my elbow.

Who can comprehend
the mystery of tables?
Between arm and chair it shifts

from stripe to woodchip,
binds in uneasy stasis
this brief quartet of stories.

*

Tank top and collar,
necktie erect and glossy
as a tulip, the right hand

adjusting a crease
beyond the artist's slow eye –
what more could one need than this?

*

Conclude with a leaf –
waxy palms streaky with rust,
stems delicate and winding

into sudden dark.
Here the day's fruit drops to earth.
Here swift, and slow, twine like light.

[CATEGORY E]

JAMES COWIE
A Portrait Group, 1933 / c.1940
GMA 1325 · Purchased 1975

25

Have You Been Crying?

by DARCY CARSON

Ribena stained sheets
Is she thinking?
Her eyelids let in no light
Is she looking?

Watching her fall
Like ringlets and curls
Watching her fall.

Ears are cold and blue
Is she listening?
I tell her about the Frisbee,
and the time the bees stung our legs,
and hot dinners in the half light,
and the sea
and

can she hear?

Watching her fall
Like ringlets and curls
Watching her fall.

Long eyelashes shimmering
Is she breathing?
Hands holding each other
Have you been crying?

Watching her fall
Like ringlets and curls
Watching her fall.

Watching her fall
Like ringlets and curls
Watching her fall.

[CATEGORY C]

EDVARD MUNCH
The Sick Girl (Das kranke Mädchen), 1896
GMA 2309 · Purchased 1981

27

The Maker

by YEVGENYA MORRISON-IGNATIEFF

Half man, half metal
A criss-cross of welded scars
He is a towering bulk of metal muscle

Sparks spray like bolts of stormy lightning
From beneath his mighty hammer
Dealt with awesome strength

Years of ash trodden down
To coat the maker's floor
But around shine the stars
Like a crown of silver light

The metal melts and bends
Beneath his practised hand
Shaping with care and attention
Unique creations grow

A metallic sheen of glory
Bathes his form with power
As he wields his tools

His forge rings and clangs
Through dawn and sunset as still he works
For joy, he does his duty

[CATEGORY A]

EDUARDO PAOLOZZI
Vulcan, 1998–9
GMA 4285 · Commissioned 1999 (with aid from the Patrons)

Kitchen

by ELLEN KENDRICK

Her hand on the glass has veins bluer than the sky, while the silent
Hum of the freezer smothers her thoughts.
Failing to open the drawer, cutlery scatters.
Clawed forks take grip on the linoleum, as spoons split
And fold. A groaning menace spreads on the kitchen floor
Handles for unseeing eyes, the corkscrew jabs
To the front, seeking out the soft flesh of her neck.

She watches her old tools crushed into the creature's crooked limbs
Scratching the walls of her lifelong habitat.
Knives curls into ribs enclosing nothing
As it scurries, a wingless fly, every motion a scrape
Of nails and blades. It crawls up her back,
Piercing the skin over her spine, its own exposed and twisted.
A cold finger closes around her neck,
The collar tightens as her fingers flounder
Against the stove, the freezer. The cutlery denies her
Air, trapped in the little room. Suffocating, the blade
Finally draws blood and her hands drop, as cold as the silver.

[CATEGORY C]

ALBERTO GIACOMETTI
Woman with her Throat Cut (Femme égorgée), 1932
GMA 1109 · Purchased 1970

31

Space, Mind, You

by SARAH McILWHAM

There is probably no such thing as space. In fact there is no such thing as space, anywhere. If you go to an empty field the first thing you do is visualise it full of people and carnival rides for your next birthday that never quite lives up to expectations. You never really have space, not in reality and not mentally.

When you come to write a piece of literature and the teacher says, 'Clear your mind,' you never truly do. You always end up wondering how long till your pen runs out or bursts, or how much the new girl's ring cost her. You end up thinking of the song you last played on your iPod or how you forgot your rubber, and how you're now doodling aimlessly love hearts and flowers on the back of your maths jotter with no means in which of erasing it. When someone says, 'Don't think about monkeys,' the first thing you do is imagine a cymbal-clapping monkey singing and dancing to an annoying holiday jingle. The process is never ending, and the point is proven: there is no such thing as mind space.

Nothing is ever empty. When you move house, the first thing you do isn't write your name on the door in swirly black lettering or introduce yourself to the neighbours, you fill it with all the junk that you swore to yourself you would get rid of but never did. Now you're having to find a place for the letter writing kit you got when you turned eighteen, the lamp that never worked and yet you still put it on display, the curtain pole you bought 'just because…'. And soon enough instead of admiring a place that has so much potential for memories, it's full of junk and soon you've run out of space and are looking to move again.

Even when you're asleep with the lumpy pillow you secretly love, you have no space; you have no clean slate on which to start anew, as somehow the neighbour's dog comes into your head and your dream, or your old teacher from nursery manages to wiggle their way into your subconscious and you never get to find out why. Some say that your brain stops growing at a certain age but how could you possibly cram in sixty years of life experiences into a brain that struggled to remember how to find the area of a sphere when you were a teen? You never spring clean your mind, get rid of the old to make space for the new, at least not intentionally; you never create space by choosing to forget. As life grows and becomes more experienced so does your mind, therefore making the possibility of space even more drastic.

There is no such thing as a blank canvas, not mentally or physically, as there is either a dirty mark in the corner or you fill it with flowers, streams and a dog without a tail. When you imagine a blank canvas or have one in front of you, with watercolour pencils at its side, you don't admire the still, the peace, the calm of the white material pulled tight over the wooden frame; you imagine the art store you walked past that had a sale on canvas paintings but you never did go in, or you are already visualising what you hope your painting will look like.

Even earth, our planet and home, has never had 'real' space before as nobody has come to a theory that the world was just emptiness. We have openness as we have miles of deserts and open seas but in them we have sand and fish and water taking up that space. Even before human existence, earth wasn't empty, there were dinosaurs, trees, bacteria, again all taking up space and taking away the possibility of complete emptiness.

When you're in the middle of writing an English essay about a boring book, without knowing or intending on having, you have an idea for your business management project. When you're being walked by the dog rather than you walking him, you remember that you must buy the same coffee beans as your friend in order to appear mature and sophisticated. Clearing your mind is almost as pointless as the task of drinking water whilst lying down, as everyone including you knows that it's going to run down your face or go up your nose or you'll begin to cough; as although you've tried, and you want to, you'll never beat the odds as it's all very pointless in trying.

So why walk into the interview empty minded, keeping the outside world at bay when it's the only thing that will keep you sane? Why not draw from experience, extract ideas from your past? Why make up a story when you have your own to tell? Why take a new sheet of paper as you have doodled on the others? Why empty your mind to go to bed when you could dream about things relative to you and who you are?

So why bother starting anew, trying to create space in your mind, wiping the slate clean, starting a fresh? – It's all just a waste of energy. All the thoughts running through your head are parts of you, and you wouldn't be you without them; so let them explode, erupt, run around free, as your mind will never be empty, or tidy, or organised so why bother pretending that its empty, or tidy or organised? So just let go. Realise that you'll always be thinking of something, so why not embrace it? Be free in your own mind, don't stare at the canvas and think of what you want it to look like, be spontaneous and artistic and creative and fill every inch of the canvas with… YOU!

[CATEGORY B]

MAN RAY
Aviary (La Volière), 1919
GMA 3888 · Purchased with the support of the
Heritage Lottery Fund and the Art Fund 1995

33

The Shape of our Family

by JESSICA MUSTARD

Bleak, black but strangely blue.
Big square Dad is being rough.
In a way, he feels so bad.
As he knows he makes me,
Small and green
Me feel so sick.

Poor Mum, a little black fearful rectangle,
Who can become a red angry rectangle.
So mad at Dad and so fearful for me.

Funny old orange, warm Gran.
Cosy and soothing to me.
Brown old Grandadpa
Like Gran,
Solid and protective.
And that's the shape of our family.

[CATEGORY A]

LYUBOV POPOVA
Painterly Architectonic, 1916
GMA 2080 · Purchased 1979

The Feast of Herod

by SELINA BUTLER-LOWRIE

The moonlight glimmered and bounced
off the solid marble flooring,
my feet moved silently, my body
swaying to the beat.
As the tune ended, I
paused, softly, holding my position.

And they rose from their seats, clapping
all around, Herod
beamed, he beamed. I
exhaled a long drawn-out breath. I'd
pleased him.

Then he rose, he rose, first
hushing his crowd, and then heaping praise.
A once in a lifetime opportunity. Something
only one can dream for. A wish.
A wish for
anything, anything I wanted.

And that's when you, who you wouldn't exactly call
the life and soul of the party, who sat obediently
in your husband's shadow, while he conducted
such events. You, the quiet one, that's when your face perked up,
your face alight, brain ticking, and I could tell you
were thinking something. Something big.

You caught me later, after the party. Sharp.
Blunt. Intimidating. Question after
question. No. I hadn't decided
yet. Yes, of course
I had thought about it.
Honestly.

It was mine though. Not yours.
But that's not the way you saw
it. You forced me, scared me to

death. I wanted to please you, didn't want
to see you so infuriated. So
I agreed.

And that was that. Not that he was too pleased though,
I guess he didn't see it coming. Isn't there something else I would like?
A pony perhaps? You were insistent though.
Give the girl what she wants Herod. Like you promised!
Your anger rose. So, like me, he too quickly caved in.

The reality of it
the power, and I knew he
was going to use it.
My wish.
Turned yours.

It was the night of praise to the Gods. He held yet another feast.
Everyone gathered, taking their seats.
The entertainment came to an end and
the crisp-suited waiters began to serve
the aperitifs. A large platter was placed in front of Herod
and the guests.

The lid was swiftly lifted, revealing
the lifeless head of John.
Cold. Stiff. Still.
Holding the same expression
as everyone in that room,
pure and utter terror.

Everyone shocked, disturbed and silent.
That is everyone, apart from you,
because you, you were smiling.
His eyes, once full of life, now seemed
dark, sinister, cold-hearted.
Like you.

CALUM COLVIN
The Feast of Herod (after Peter Paul Rubens), 1998

Here's To

by NIAMH FRANCIS

Here's to the fast times, the times we felt alive. Here's to the nights that we forgot to get back home. Here's to the dresses and the discos, to every girl we saw and caught a feel of in the crowds. Here's to the empty bottles and the memories we've lost. Here's to the cocktails and every sunrise we fell asleep to, the innocence we eagerly drank away. Here's to every strange bed and bed-mate, to the lies we were cocooned in like the sheets of each one-night stand. Here's to the girls you know you left with nothing but stains and the sunrise through the windowpane. Here's to what we've lost.

Drink up now, drink up. It's up she comes and down she goes. Drink to the party scene; it's won. It's got the best of me and you.

We were nocturnal, revelling in the starlight, or, better, the pumping strobes. So tired that we were brainless, yet more alive than the rest of the mundane world. Safe was a curse-word, an impossibility, an idea we hated more than anything else. We hounded it out with drugs and madness, crazed dreams and reckless actions that chased 'safe' away. You and me ran like madmen through the streets and clubs and fights and girls, the days and nights that blur to one demented dance of ecstasy.

Knock it back now; it's your last shot. Make it a toast to your favourite addictions, the calls that you can still feel through your dead nerve cells and burned out nose. Cruelty, depravity, infliction, torture – it's so much more fun when you do it to yourself.

Here's to the times you couldn't feel your heartbeat, when the bass was stronger than you were. Here's to life behind novelty sunglasses, life beneath mullet wigs and choking cigarette smoke. Here's to the broken dreams in our screwed up heads, the ones where we never died and just kept freaky-dancing, past the dawn and into Revelations. Here's to every pair of shoes and leather limo sofa we puked on. Here's to the nights when we couldn't find our souls. Here's to the days when we're still looking for them. Here's to every woman who ever told us to drop dead, and the ones who didn't get to say it to our faces. You know they hope you choke on this last drink, every one of them. They're getting their wish.

We're dying now, the both of us. You worried about your sins? The lies of love and tricks you played, the whores you used and the other girls you didn't pay – they're the worst, so fresh, so young, so sweet as you slipped those things into their drinks. The theft and the coveting, the parents you forgot, the chemicals you worshipped, the Sabbaths you tripped out on… Got any regrets? I didn't think so.

If I could start again I'd have it different – better. Worse. Faster, brighter, wilder, harder, more drink, more drugs, more sex, more parties, starting younger, ending older – not ending until the very end. I'd have thrown away my inhibitions before I let them hold me back, dived straight into the ocean before I stopped to dip my toes. I'd have squandered all my savings; I wouldn't have tried to change, wasting less time, less government money on the counselling I knew couldn't help me from the start. I would never have let them stop me eating my face from the inside out.

I think we knew, from the start, that that was us, forever. We knew the trap was closing as we threw down our house of cards, but you never looked up so I never did. I never looked up so you never did. We were sucked into that world by our youth and weakness, spinning our own whirlpool as we let it drag us down. It's a wave that you can ride if you let it sweep you on. Don't fight, just party, ride the wave to your untimely end. Because when you try to turn back, that's when you start drowning.

That's us, we're drowning now. We're playing our hand with one chip left. How could we think we had so little to lose? Because we had it, clear as the daylight we never saw, and we lost it.

It's just you and me now. You, me and these curtains, these two beds, these two last drinks. The doctors don't know we

have them, but this is how we want to go. No bangs or whimpers, just the ringing in our ears and the drugs in our throats, bond in our hearts and the burned out holes in our livers. I raise my glass, and you raise yours.

Here's to the fast times, the times we felt alive. Here's to the nights we forgot to get back home. A toast to the party scene; it's won. It's got the best of me and you.

I swallow.

DAVID WILLIAMS
Michael Clark, 1989

PGP 117.5 · Commissioned by the Scottish National Portrait Gallery in 1988

Paint

by JOSEPH REED

You know me: I'm often covered with paint. So when I hear this fuckwit, Chris, call me Mr Paint, while I'm through in the kitchen mixing up a protein shake, I just take a few deep breaths and say to myself: 'Hey, he's got a point.'

At that time I did not bring up the fact here he was, Chris, in my sitting room, talking to my wife, calling *me* Mr Paint. I did not, either, observe that I had *not once* made mention of him always wearing wool, or that he had that strange metallic smell of old men who live alone. *Never* can it be said that I called him Mr Wool or Mr Tincan.

I just picked up my bike, rolled it along the hallway and rode it down the steps and out into the street.

Next time, then, when Chris is round, on the sofa, talking to my wife about narrative arcs, I come in. Guess what? I'm covered in paint. Chris says, 'Still painting the Forth Bridge?' I am aware of the moral high ground, I am aware of the boundaries; the kind which Chris likes to discuss 'in the abstract', so I say, 'Yes, look at me: I'm covered in paint.'

I am not adverse to admitting something which is obvious, not even in my own home.

The week after that, I'm coming back from a job and I'm all covered in paint. I get in and I stamp my boots, I unbolt my door, I wrestle my dog, I sit down with my wife and we have a cup of tea. We start talking about that particular renovation, then we begin to talk about the next week's work, which is doing a patio. Then my wife says to me, 'Oh good, that will be a change, I'm tired of you always being covered in paint.'

I don't know much, apart from how to make a patio and how to clean off paint, but I do know that nothing happens three times without a good reason. I also know that my wife has never before had a problem with me being covered with paint. I think, 'Chris, you are a motherfucker.'

I go round to the University. I do not have a student card and I do not look like a student. I do have a van full of ladders, however, and a good idea of where Chris's office is, having stopped off to watch him go to work before my job started. I can separate my thoughts and my emotions, but when what is true and what I feel come together I am very potent.

I climb on to the roof of the lecture theater. I do an army crawl towards the window of the first-floor corridor. I put both hands against the pane and I slide it up from the outside.

Chris's door has his full name on it, Christopher, like his book jackets. I knock on the door. I am not the kind of man to kick down a door if I do not have to. Chris says, 'Come on in,' in his voice – that voice – as if the very act of talking is boring to him.

When Chris sees me he says, 'Hello John.' I am out of breath from crawling across the roof and my front is black with roofing tar. 'You're covered in paint,' says Chris, mistaking the tar for paint.

'You know me,' I say, massaging my hands, preparing, 'I'm Mr Paint.'

[CATEGORY D]

WILLIAM JOHNSTONE
Embryonic, 1972–3
GMA 3563 · Bequeathed by Mrs Hope Montagu Douglas Scott 1990

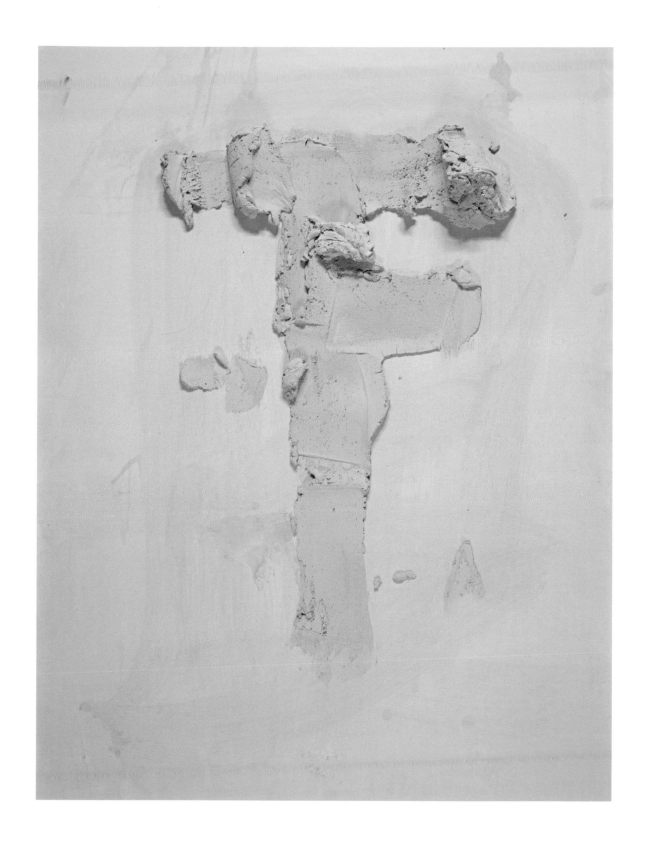

Moon Halo

by JOSEPHINE BROGAN

Dominating the dank, sunk garden and the narrow
path to the kitchen door, the halo'd moon put
all our peevish thoughts to flight. We stopped, in awe
at such a vision. Happens sometimes, the moon's light

refracting as it travels through high wisps of cloud – cirrus
spread in a puff-ball skirt, a colossal shawl. A cuirass
made from crystalled ice. This circle of unearthly
grandeur hung huge over the town and I thought of lowly

shepherds, biblical kings. Of a halo'd babe and his
innocent mother. Of all the mothers rising from
a fraught bed to tiptoe in, who'd see it and pause
in wonder. Then turn to check, tuck in an arm

or leg – each child his own, halooing off the steep
cliffs, lording it in the avenues, of sleep.

[CATEGORY E]

DAMIEN HIRST
Beautiful C Painting, 1996
GMA 4477 · Purchased 2002

43

If You Go Down to the Woods Today …

by ANNIE FORBES

Susie runs. A dinosaur is chasing her. Its claws skitter and crunch on the museum stairs and she can feel hot breath on her neck. She shrieks with laughter and clatters into the next room. She stops in her tracks. The imaginary monster is forgotten, and it stalks back to its exhibit, dragging its slithery tail down the steps.

There is a wet, shiny nose staring at her. Above it, a pair of tiny crinkly eyes, like currants, are buried in a mass of honey brown fur. Susie's thumb creeps up to her mouth.

She stares at the thing in the case, and the thing stares back. A bear.

'Hey,' murmurs the bear. Susie eyes him warily. He sneezes violently, wipes his eyes, and beckons to her.

'Come over here, kid.'

He has a weary American drawl to his words. His voice is deep and syrupy, and he sounds like he has a blocked nose. Susie doesn't move. The bear begins to hum, and then to mutter under his breath:

> 'Look for the bare necessities,
> The simple bare necessities,
> Forget about your worries and your strife…'

The bear doesn't look like he's from *The Jungle Book*. His coat is shabby and he stares reproachfully up from under a furrowed brow. He's no Baloo. Susie edges forward, as if she is approaching a strange dog. She sinks to her knees, glancing at his paws. Paws the size of dustbin lids. The singing trails off as girl and bear study each other.

Susie sees a small ghost girl with blonde hair reflected in the glass. The girl is wearing Susie's favourite red jumper, and her black stamping boots. She imagines living with the bear, looking out at all the people visiting the museum. It would be hard to keep still all day, but the attendant would bring them bread and honey, and let them out after closing time. She wonders if her mum would come and see her, sometimes.

'Where do you come from, bear?' whispers the girl. She places her palm to the cool glass, leaving a misty hand shape.

The bear looks up sharply, then he lowers his head and begins to trace a pattern on the dusty floor. His fur bristles and his hackles rise ever so slightly. He is remembering the last winter of his life, before he woke up to this eternal season of central heating and dust.

…There isn't enough to eat and his children are starving and crying out for meat, so he crosses the bleak wastelands and heads for a huddle of concrete grey buildings. Human territory. He is big and fearless and ambling along with a swagger in his step. He starts to rummage around the dump on the outskirts of the town, searching for food. He gets lucky, and his paw is lodged in a vat of salted herrings when there is a shout, and a sour odour drifting in the air.

'Hey, bear!'

He raises his head, spattered with fish scales. A man strides towards him, arm outstretched. The light winks off something metal concealed in the man's hand. A scorching hot taste explodes in the bear's throat, mixing with the salt tang of brine…

He coughs and raises his eyes from the floor. 'Me? That takes me back. Alaska, little girl. Alaska. It's big and brutal and beautiful. The wind is cold, and the earth is black, and the air tastes like pine needles.'

The girl breathes out. 'Oh.'

Her face is pressed right up to the glass, and her breath is making hot little clouds on the surface.

'My name is Susie. I'm from 37 Woodhill Road, Edinburgh, Scotland, EH14 3RB. I have a yellow cat, and my door is blue.'

The bear's eyes are twinkling. He sits on his haunches, facing the girl.

'Are you a dancing bear?' she asks.

WENDY MCMURDO
Girl with Bears, Royal Museum of Scotland, Edinburgh, 1999
GMA 4310 · Purchased (Iain Paul Fund) 1999

The animal chuckles to himself, a sound like pebbles falling into a stream. Once, he was brushed and disinfected, and his door was left ajar...

A saggy, slightly moth eaten bear waltzes drunkenly in a darkened museum. His belly hangs in pouches, like trousers a size too big, and he sways from side to side, eyes closed in ecstasy, shuffling round the empty halls and deserted exhibits. There's a solo trumpet and the tinkle of piano ringing out in his head as he slides discreetly down a banister.

The bear collides with a display of ancient pottery, grooves beneath the bleached bones of a blue whale, and sashays past a troop of Roman soldiers who look on in envy. His claws click and slide on the polished floor.

The air is stale, and he drinks it in like wine.

In the morning he has to be dragged back to his case, claws scratching grooves on the marble floor. His captor sweats and swears inside his uniform, muttering about practical jokes. Wrestling with a

stubborn stuffed bear, who seems to have a mind of its own.

'Of course not,' the bear snickers, a sly smile rippling his furry jaws. 'I have no one to dance with. The bear beside me? She's stuffed. Can't you see that?' He waves a paw in front of the smaller animal's face. 'See? Nothing. Nada. Sleeping beauty.'

'Then, don't you have a friend?' Susie whispers. 'I do. Her name is Karen and she can run round my house six times without stopping. Her hair is black, and she has braces, but her teeth are white. I don't think she talks to bears in museums. Especially real ones.'

'To tell you the truth little girl, it gets pretty lonesome in here. Those jackals over there are plain crazy, and all the possum does is chew on his own tail. The critter's a loon. As for the owl, he just twists his head on his neck, round and round, and watches you with those big mournful eyes of his. The cheetah's a snob. Sometimes the whale talks to me, though. Well, he sings…'

Susie is listening to every word. Entranced. She smiles shyly. She wonders if the bear could carry her like her dad used to, before she got too big. The bear's back is hunched and his fur sticks up in tufts. It would tickle her, she thinks. Like feathers in a pillow.

'Your fur needs a brush,' she informs him. 'It's all messy.'

'Hey, I'm not a teddy bear, you know.' The animal grins. He smudges his nose up to the glass, and it's his turn to leave a sticky heart shaped print on the pristine surface. Museum attendants don't clean on the inside. He steals a glance at Susie, who gazes up at him expectantly. She wants him to sing to her again. A sigh swells in his chest. The girl has stirred memories deep inside of him, and homesickness churns in his gut. He misses *everything*.

…A river rushes past his paws, its icy currents tugging him downstream. A cub wriggles and squeals as he closes his jaws gently round the scruff of its neck, dunks it under the water, and licks its fur into clean little spikes. Later, it cuffs at his ears with tiny paws. Revenge. An osprey is calling across the ice, and the salmon are leaping. Steaming pink flesh, and honey sweet blood bursting down his throat. Hot, vital fluid, flooding his veins. Pooling, congealing, healing. Coils of breath curling round his snout. A heartbeat in his chest. The sky. Stars…

46   A scar, roughly stitched like a seam, runs the length of the

bear's body. He traces it with a claw. Susie looks on, wide eyed. The ghost girl inside the glass is suddenly dwarfed by the hulking beast beside her. It could hurt her. It could gobble her up.

'Hey, goldilocks,' smirks the bear. 'Did you eat all my porridge?' He opens his wide, red ridged mouth. White teeth emerge in a hollow, cavernous yawn of a laugh. The girl in the case taps hard on the glass, mouthing something to Susie. She can't get out. She's trapped.

The bear's laugh is warped by the shield of glass and it echoes out bitterly. His eyes are black slits of sorrow in a lopsided cage of a head. Susie flinches back and gets to her feet. Things that hide under the bed, in gun barrels and in grownups' heads, are hiding in the dead bear's eyes. She stumbles blindly, clawing tears from her eyes as she runs, abandoning her reflection. The ghost girl vanishes. The twinkle-eyed bear is left behind in the darkened room.

The museum is too big, and Susie is too small. The floor stretches for miles, and she's running, running…

Straight into the arms of her mother.

'Hey Susie, what's wrong? Did you get lost?' Her mum envelopes her in a soft, perfumed hug. Safe. Susie sobs happily into her chest.

'Come on sweetie. You're a big, brave girl now. Come and see the giraffes.'

Susie is clutching onto her mother's skirt, like she did when she was younger. The folds of material feel soft and comforting in her fingers. Everything is alright. She prattles away about Alaska to her mum. They did a project on it in school…

The bear watches Susie go. He cranes his neck, desperate not to lose sight of her. She rounds the corner and he's no longer a bear.

It's a skin, stuffed with wire, wood and foam. It smells slightly of mothballs and preservative. A thin film of dust coats the cold surfaces of the two chips of glass lodged in its head. Stuffed bears don't cry. They don't even blink, but like a painting, if you dig deep enough beneath their skin, you'll find a story. They can't sneeze or weep or dance or sing, but they can't forget, either. They're alive.

[CATEGORY B]

Tusitala

by AILEEN BALLANTYNE

It was not the place of my birth that I loved,
nor the trail of her smoke nor the sun on the Forth;
nor the dark of her light nor her half-light;

but this land I have found,
and the splash and the roar of her sea,

where the women take the hair from their heads
to weave bamboo-grass mosaics
and the ink dries on my pen as I write.

I stand now on a hillside
By the sweet vanilla planted,
and her people are my people;

I remember, now and then,
the pale light of the North:
its soot-black towers
and razored dusk-black steeples
etched out in silhouette,
and the counterpane coughed-red
as I lay in bed, dreaming
paper-chains of islands in my head.

It was not the place of my birth that I loved,
but this land I have found,
where they call me *Tusitala*,
and I breathe with the sea.

[CATEGORY D]

COUNT GIROLAMO NERLI
Robert Louis Stevenson, 1892
PG 847 · Bequeathed by Mrs Turnbull 1915

Street Kids

by PHILIP MURNIN

The baby was early. It shouldn't have been here until Halloween but it was only September and on its way. We were eating Sunday Shepherd's Pie, when mam went white and stared at her lap as if she was saying a prayer. She whispered oh like she'd made a spill and she stood up. On her pinny was redness. We stared at the growing red spot. It was as if her pinny was flowering – a red rose growing between her legs. And we sat with our forks halfway to our mouths and watched it. Paddy thought she'd only spilled the beetroot but it was coming from mam. She told us the baby was coming and sent Paddy to get feyther.

We weren't allowed into Rottenrow, feyther said, so we stayed back on Kennedy Street to wait on the baby. It was Sunday and after dinner so the street was dead. Davie McClure came to join us because he wasn't wanted at home. He slunk about the streets from morning until night.

The three of us went to see the painter in her studio – a big white room except where she'd spilled paint. Which was most places including her clothes. We told her that our wee baby brother was being born and that we were to help name it. She asked how we knew it was a boy and we told her that granny tested mam's belly with a wedding ring.

'How absolutely wonderful,' the painter said and went away and came back with a name book for us to look at while we waited for the baby. She said that I must bring the baby and she might paint it. I told her I would have to see and she laughed. I saw one of her paintings once – one of some children. The baby better not look like that.

We took the name book with us back out to the street. Paddy wanted to call it Patrick. What a daftie! You couldn't have two brothers called Patrick. People would say the Murrays were eejits. He just wanted the baby to be called wee Paddy so he could be big Paddy. He felt bad because I was taller than him even though he was a year older and a boy.

Davie said that he thought that Alexander was a nice name but me and Paddy told him to shut up. He wasn't allowed to choose because he wasn't the baby's brother or sister and nobody had told him that he could help name the baby. He was just here because he wasn't wanted at home.

The book said that Catherine meant 'pure'. Pure Murray. Not just a bit Murray, pure Murray. That was me. I told Paddy that my name meant pure and he said there must be a word missing in the book.

'How?' I asked.

'Cos it should say – pure eejit.'

So he got hit. Patrick's name meant noble but he wasn't noble because he was always picking his nose and flicking it at me. So when he asked what his name meant, I put on a voice as if I was reading it off the page and told him that it meant little flower. That kept him quiet for a while.

Davie didn't know that names meant things. I told him, David meant beloved.

He said, 'That can't be right.'

So I showed him and he said that his mammy couldn't have known that names had meanings either. He was right. Davie McClure wasn't wanted at home. It just went to show that names were a lot of rubbish.

But the baby needed a good one definitely. Alexander meant Man's Defender. Man's Defender Murray. I couldn't wait to put the baby in the pram and take it out in the evenings to show people and to the likes of Lizzie Hamilton, I'd say,

'This is my wee brother…Sandy… Isn't he bonny? He'll grow up to be a Man's Defender.'

Lizzie would ask for a hold and I would say, 'Certainly not. I wouldn't want Sandy getting any germs.'

I couldn't get the redness on the pinny out of my head. What if there was something wrong? Paddy said it was simple business. The baby grew and when it was big enough, it came out the bum.

'But the red spot, Paddy,' I said.

Davie McClure said it wasn't simple. His mammy's baby had died. Now she couldn't have any more.

'That's because yous didn't look after it properly,' Paddy got him told.

He didn't reply. It was true. The McClures weren't decent like the Murrays. Davie had knitting needle legs sticking out his shorts and his skin was stretched tight and white. His knees were screwed on like bed knobs. Davie didn't even wear socks and the gaps between soles and shoes snapped together like a pair of crocodiles' mouths. He sometimes chased me with his crocodiles and I screamed even though it was just shoes.

The sun was a huge red spot in the sky and the moon was a pale slit – a sideways smirk. It would soon be the first day of the baby's life. I saw feyther coming down the empty street.

I waved but he ignored me. I skipped up Kennedy Street and I shouted, 'Is it a wee boy then? If it is it's to be called Alexander. It means Man's Defender.'

I skipped round feyther singing, '*Mans Def-en-der Alex-ander Mens de-fander Alex–an-der Alex-fander Mens den-an-der.*'

Feyther only said wheesht. He strode straight down Kennedy Street and didn't stop when I tripped on the cobbles. Into the darkness of the close, he strode and never said a word. I watched him from where I fell. My knee was skint and bleeding. I sat and hugged it. It tasted of salt and metal. Me and Paddy didn't want to follow him into the darkness of the close so we stayed out on the street with Davie McClure.

[CATEGORY D]

JOAN EARDLEY
*Street Kids, c.*1949–51
GMA 887 · Purchased with funds given
by an anonymous donor 1964

Imagine You are Driving

by GUINEVERE GLASFURD-BROWN

I started out with the others on a boat from Kismayo. They are gone and my family is gone and now I am on a bus in England with children like me. The bus goes where it goes without slowing. There are no checkpoints, no barricades. No one tries to stop us or climbs on board with a bomb. The driver will not be beaten with sticks or made to dance before he is shot. At night, we drive with many lights and all our driver wants to do is sing. He leans across and turns up the radio. *Papapapapapapokafay*, *papapapapapapokafay*, he sings, louder each time, and rests a hand on his leg.

Outside, the sky is dark and the road is black. I sink lower in my seat. I cannot stop shaking.

The children like me they call unacompanee. They put me next to a small boy but he looked at me as if I had snakes in my pockets and cried so hard that they had to move him. Now one of the uniforms sits with me instead. It is not good to stare but his skin is strange. He is hairy and heavy, but not strong. My Commander was not fat. His arms were not soft. He had food for me until he didn't and anyway his dogs could not stand by then and they had no strength left to bark.

This day there has been more rain than could fill the well. 'Allahu Akbar,' I say and the uniform stabs a finger at me and says, 'No funny business.' He looks at me and repeats this more slowly, like it's a command, 'No funny business, you hear?'

I say, 'No, boss,' and he folds his arms and closes his eyes. I watch him. He pretends to sleep. The bus drives on and the rain falls.

'Boss,' I say, but his eyes stay shut. It is not wise to shake a uniform. In the end I have no choice. I wet myself.

He tells the driver to stop at the next services, and the bus pulls in by a red and yellow sign that is as tall as a palm tree. '*Mistermacdonal!*' a child cries out as the deep red light moves across each of us in turn. We press our cheeks up against the glass and then turn to each other, our open mouths a line of amazed circles. Then the light goes and the shadow pulls a black hood over us one by one.

'Filthy,' the man says as he scrubs my seat. 'Five minutes,' he tells the driver and marches me off the bus.

'Boss,' I say and I tug on his sleeve. I point to a sign where the bus had turned.

He jerks his arm free. 'Immigration Reception Centre. Fifteen miles. Not far.' He walks away, and then calls back over his shoulder, 'Oi! This way.'

Outside the toilet there is a small, dark space with tall machines and bright lights. One man holds on to a machine. He holds it as if it is his. He has a hand either side, at hip height, and presses the buttons hard. Something catches the uniform's eye. He pushes me towards the toilet and says, 'Get changed, then straight back.'

After I change and wash my hands I come back out and he is sitting in front of one of the machines. I watch him, and press my cheek against the cold, black surface. He stares at the TV in the machine and pushes a coin into a slot with his thumb. The picture jumps then starts to move, opening up a wide road. It is confusing. The white lines in the centre move towards me but the lines at the sides move away. He rests his hands on a wheel and drives. The corners are long and sometimes sharp and he drives faster and faster and he does not blink or smile. He says, 'Haven't done this in years.'

I don't have the words for what I want to say to him.

The machine clicks and the road disappears and he sits there. 'I wonder where it goes?' he says after a while. I shrug.

'You ever had a go with one of these?' he asks as he levers himself out of the seat. He digs in one pocket. 'Here. Imagine you are driving…' and he pushes me with a nudge towards the machine, his other hand is open and inviting. As I lower myself onto the seat, he drops a coin into the slot and I hold the wheel. The road flickers before me and starts to curve and the curve goes on and on and is long and black and the sky is blue and clear like the sky above Mogadishu.

'Where are you driving?' he asks.

The first word in my head is the wrong word. I turn a tight

JULIAN OPIE
Imagine You are Driving I, 1998?
GMA 4349 · Presented by the Contemporary Art Society 2000

corner with a flick of the wheel and then turn in the opposite direction. My heart beats faster. 'New York,' I say.

He thinks this is funny and laughs.

'New York,' I repeat and I grip the wheel tighter.

For a while we both stare at the screen as if expecting New York to appear around the next bend. Then he looks at his watch. 'That's it. Time's up.'

I shake my head.

'The road goes wherever you want it to, kid,' he says.

Does he think I am stupid? I know it goes nowhere other than the back of the machine and behind that there's not even space for me to squeeze in.

'Out,' he says. He pulls me so hard that my arms go up and bend back behind my head. As he drags me away I see the wheel spin out of control. The road does not care. It curves and curves and moves on without me.

Lament for a Tiger (1926)

by ANNIE FORBES

I am Elephant, Sister Elephant.
Slave to spurs on tender ears.
Brother cringes in the gloaming,
silent as his death skulks near.

Blazing firework in the night,
Proud one, Wild one, dogged, bled,
dying in the red dawn light.

Extinguished.
Frantic.
Hiss of fright.

Ponderous traitors, heads bent humble,
ring of tusks, our kin's defeat.
Ammonite trunks unfurl and fumble.
Embroidered elephants gently weep.

We are Beaters, Nameless Beaters,
numbers swell like ants or flies.
Swarming forward.
Drums and cymbals
mingle with our lowly cries.

Mr Tiger, cruel and cunning.
Lurking shadow
in disguise.

We are vermin, we are many,
fill the jungle with our song.
Taunted, spat at, eyes averted.
Dirty like a pack of dogs.

Without us,
Sirs you would be stranded.
Tobacco grins on sinners' lips.

If we catch you gold striped treasure
Gracious Lady,
will you tip?

We are Rajas, Rolls Royce Rajas.
Maharajas if you please.
Downwind of the broody kitten,
opium smoke drifts through the leaves.

Opals nestle in our turbans,
tokens of our obscene wealth.
These bumbling, stumbling, blasted British,
know nothing of a hunter's stealth:

Helmets crowning ruddy features,
malaria, breeches, jutting knees.
We'll frolic with these clumsy tourists
Line their pockets with rupees.

Because, despite their pompous husbands
See the fair-skinned, dainty wives?
Sporting bright blue British bloodlines
(charming ladies, lovely lies.)

We are Masters, British Masters.
Mother India whimpers. Falls.
We are Men and we will Conquer
beast and country, one and All.

We'll mount the head up in the parlour
flies sup satin, sacred blood.
The coolies flay the feral king,
savage in a surging flood.

Dignity and waxed moustaches,
Dominion, Valour and Prestige,
Tiger trembles, watch us saunter,
quash the beast in time for Tea…

I am Tiger.
Noble Tiger.
Crumpled husk at Masters' feet.

Tacky trophy, once Elite
now Empty Emperor of the East.

Paw prints fleeting, phantom feline
bolting through the afternoon.
Tracked and baited, grazed by muskets,
lost in brush, the red sky blooms.

Teased and tortured through the moonlight,
Ragged wraith melts in the sun.
Smoked out mewling, staggering blindly,
snuffed point blank by an eager gun.

Rabid, raving, hungry hunters,
Circle for a Glorious Kill.

Seeping slowly through the foliage,
Coppery death breaths rasp
Until

knives slice quick.
A deity dies.
Wretched ruby gizzards dry.

A regal,
smouldering,
tawny prize.
Who can look me in the eye?

[CATEGORY B]

LESLIE HAMILTON WILSON

The Tiger. H.H. Guests and Beaters, c.1926

PGP 236.160 · Purchased 1998

The Colour of Sorrow

by IONA BYRNE

1

You stare at me
through empty, grainy eyes.

Sitting straight-
backed you glare
at my back as
I turn my face away.

I sit in my
chair and sigh, a
sound so familiar
it feels like security.

Your lips graze
my cheek and
I feel your eyes
burning.

Lips on mine
sweet and sure,
filled with passion
and lust.

I picture you
cold and alone
clutching my letters,
listening to death.

2

The neighbour's house exploded late
one night,
shrapnel flying across the
familiar field,
scattering into the dark
to join the stars and the
broken promise.

3

I'll send you socks
and cigarettes
and a letter that
you'll read.
Tears on cheap paper
poisoned with my
scrawling print.

I'll tell you that
I miss you and
the baby's doing fine.
I'll moan about
the lack of milk
and try to pass the
time, filling every
inch with words of
tender love.

I won't say
every night I sob and
hold your picture close
as the sky lights up
and the house shakes.

[CATEGORY C]

ROBERT HENDERSON BLYTH
'Existence Precarious', 1946
PG 2851 · Purchased with money from the Knapping Fund 1991

Allegory

by HEATHER REID

It was the year the light changed: the days were brighter, hotter, the nights alive with aurora borealis as far south as The Needles. There was talk of a second coming, you couldn't move for Jesus freaks pointing to the signs, although by then any idiot could have walked on water, the algae was so dense: curds of it piled against the shore and harbour walls. Folk began to leave, even those whose roots stretched back for generations; they sold up what they could and went to look for work inland. Nobody blamed them, the sea was dead and there seemed little point in hanging on.

At night you could almost forget. Lights still burned in the cottages and the water looked black as it should. True, the sound was different: a muffled slump rather than the whispered hiss of waves, but, if you took the back road to the inn, rather than the coastal path, you could kid yourself that things were still okay.

That evening I followed the shore, tossing pebbles out into the water. Archie was sitting on the jetty, the tip of his roll-up glowing in the dark. His was the last boat in the harbour, the others long since burnt or given up for salvage. One or two had been beached and left to rot and their wooden ribs arched in the sand like the carcasses of great whales. 'She's a brave girl,' I said, pointing to the Margaret Ann, 'last of her kind.'

'Aye, you're not wrong.' Archie flicked the butt of his fag into the sea and I heard it fizzle. There was a sense of desolation, a silence unnatural even for night. 'I'm taking her out.'

We walked to the inn and I stood him a malt or two, the burn of peat fierce in our throats. The landlord, John, was an artist who'd come to our village to paint the way of life. That was twenty years ago. *Now I only draw pints* he'd quip, although there was little humour in the words. I told him Archie's plan.

'You're wasting your time, my friend,' said John, 'there's nothing left. What the nets didn't take the algae smothered. I'd put my faith in whisky, if I were you; less chance of disappointment. What'll it be?'

Archie frowned and shook his head. 'You're wrong,' he said.

JOHN BELLANY *Allegory*, 1964
GMA 3359 · Purchased 1988

It was an especially dark night, cloudy and starless, as we followed Archie down to his boat. We both knew it was foolish, dangerous even, but we helped him cast off, then watched as the Margaret Ann ironed a shimmering blue crease of bio-luminescence into the black velvet fabric of the sea. I remember feeling sick but John lifted his hand to wave, and called, 'good luck, mate,' as the vessel disappeared.

Days passed and word of Archie's leaving spread around the village. An unofficial vigil began. People took turns to stand on the headland, scanning the verdant seascape for a boat. Even the children joined in, filtering down to the harbour after school or cycling up the coast road to the point. I took my turn in the evenings, straining my eyes against the fading autumn sunlight. Ahead, Bass Rock rose like the crown of a wide-brimmed hat, long since deserted by the guillemots and solant geese that once formed a blizzard round the island: no fish, we learned, no birds.

It was around 7pm when I caught sight of the boat. Tilda McClaverty and her wee lad, Mattie, had come to keep me company and we shared a poke of chips from Chas's chip bar. Even from a distance I could see something was wrong, the Margaret Ann was sitting low in the water though her bow rose high and proud. Whatever she was towing was pulling her back end down and furrowing the algae like a plough. As she drew nearer I could hear her engine labouring against the weight. 'Go tell the others,' I said to Mattie, 'and tell them to be quick, I think there's fish.'

They came with their tools, those that were left: the netters and gutters, the flensers and scalers, all standing on the harbour when Archie moored the boat. 'You'll need the crane,' he shouted and Eck ran to bring it round. There was excitement and a sense of hopeful expectation as Archie secured the catch but I saw in his face they were misguided: his skin was waxen and his eyes dulled by horror. When at last the fish were landed I saw why.

What can I tell you about those fish? There were three of them, each as monstrous as the next, their huge bodies swollen with disease, their skins laced with sores and lacerations. But it was their heads that sickened, grotesque in the dying light, ribbons of flesh hanging from their gills, their saucer-eyes white and blind. People turned away, I heard Tilda say to Mattie, 'Go on home, son,' knowing, as I suspect we all did, that nightmares lay ahead. After that, silence, then someone spat and Eck moved forward, took a flensing tool from his neighbour and began to hack until each ruined head had been removed. He stood, panting, working his jaw as if to keep himself from crying. Then, when I could stand it no longer, I pushed through the crowd and kicked those heads into the harbour, watching as the swaying green algae closed, like lips, around them.

I don't remember whose idea it was to crucify the fish, only that it took eight men to lift them. The crosses erected for a passion play three years ago had remained there ever since, as if somehow we had known they had a purpose still to serve. The men worked quickly, slitting a knife along each belly and opening them out as though preparing them for drying. After that the innards were hosed away and the bodies hoisted up to the cross-beam and hammered on. When the work was done, Archie stood beneath the sagging fish and, rubbing a hand across his face, announced, 'That's all of them. It's finished.' Tilda began to cry and I pulled her to my chest and held her close.

We stood like that for hours until the moon rose fat and yellow and Bass Rock glowed like a halo behind the fish. From somewhere in the crowd there came the sound of someone praying. John, called from the inn, began to sketch.

[CATEGORY E]

JOHN BELLANY detail from *Allegory*, 1964
GMA 3359 · Purchased 1988

Life of a Slave

by KEIR OGILVY

Before 'this' happened,
He was a happy man,
A family man,
Content.
But now,
His dreams are shattered.

All day,
Every day,
Is spent in those fields.
Every …
Waking …
Moment …
Down he goes.
Like a boat descending into the depths.
He can't go on like this.

No one saw him fall.
He looks around,
Still no one takes any notice.
Slowly he drags
His slim scabby body along the ground.
Like an old car he rasps and splutters.

Squeezing through a hole in the fence,
He shuts his eyes, and runs,
The hills, the countryside,
Anywhere,
Just away.

He was caught,
Betrayed,
Dragged back.
Back 'there'.
Back to hell.

Waiting for his punishment.
The overseer taunting him.
The suck up,
The Beelzebub.
He's called in.
The farmer's there.
A smile on his face,
The whip in his hand.
1 … 2 … 3 … 4 … 5,
He was being torn apart,
Piece by piece.
101 … 102 … 103 …
Pride was the only thing holding back the tears,
197 … 198 … 199 … 200 …
The beatings subsided.
The farmer's wife whimpering in the corner,
Hopelessly pleading for his life.

[CATEGORY A]

ANTONIO PISANELLO (DI PUCCIO PISANO)
Study of a Young Man with his Hands Tied behind his Back,
*c.*1434–8
D 722 · David Laing Bequest to the Royal Scottish Academy 1878;
transferred to the National Gallery 1910

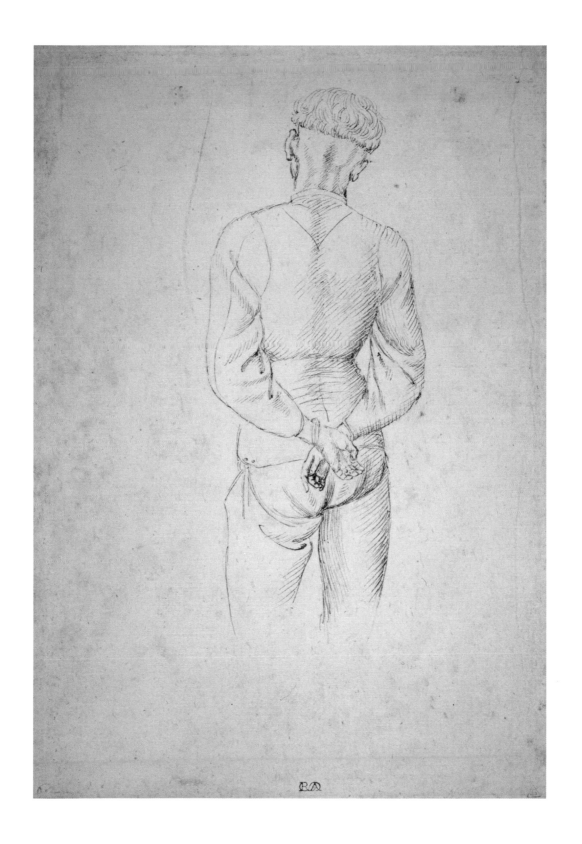

Reflection

by ZOE STORRIE

Spring has come and he
is alone –
around him are others
yet he is alone, existing between them.

His eyes snap from the river
to the cotton mill,
far away, yet tall, imposing.
In the sea of his mind, memories float, resurfacing:
thick cotton dust, thicker coughs,
spinning, both cotton and himself from the heat
and the noisy hum – a bee in his eardrum.
He will not return,
not to the ten and three hours each day
nor to the nostril clinging smell
causing sneeze upon sneeze.

A splash sounds
to his left
and he returns
to the river.

A romance begins
between his sockless feet and the grass:
long strands like ribbons of silk
twist around and tickle his toes,
toes squeezing tight
keeping them there, their green playmate
for one second, two
before flattening them again.

A boy of eight or nine
is humming softly
as if copying the river's rhythm.
It was he that caused the sobering
splash.

With busy hands as small as they are strong,
he washes his black beauty,
more than a foal, not quite yet a mare.
Small waterfalls run from her and
she is glittering,
her raven coat a blanket of minuscule diamonds
catching the rays of the sun.

The silver river has become
a rainbow –
reflections of azure sky,
grass more emerald than green
and running from the muddy horse
warm red and brown,
like the underbelly of a thousand salmon.

In the wise and slowly blinking eye
of the sparkling horse
he catches a glimpse of himself,
solemn and calm
like the clouds floating above,
flirting with the sun and birds.
It is then, under the leafy shade
It comes to him, the realisation
That he is not a factory boy,
or a child
like the one before him,
but a man,
hopeful and unyielding.

[CATEGORY C]

GEORGES SEURAT

*A Study for 'Une Baignade', c.*1883

NG 2222 · Presented by Sir Alexander Maitland in memory of his wife Rosalind 1960

Cornfields at Nightfall

by LAURA HELYER

Evening is happening, the light settles down
slowly to the colours of shadows, the warm air
made buoyant and full with fragrance.
We hear fields of meadow buttercup and poppy,
the breeze making the long grass water
and smoke as the hare speeds through it.
Now the cornfields are finished,
sore from the harvest, the earth loosened.

It is the red sea she wants to remember,
this vermilion bleeding under the dusking sky,
where the moon fills its bowl with chalk
and the night tempers and falls.
See how the paint soaks down into the act
of remembrance, recovers the shocks
through the earth and shows them:
here are rubies, here are tombs of crimson.

[CATEGORY D]

JOAN EARDLEY
Summer Fields, *c.*1961
GMA 2940 · Bequeathed by Mr R.R. Scott Hay and presented by Mrs M.E.B. Scott Hay 1984

The Plot

by JAMIE ARNAUD

Unlike most monkeys I have always been intrigued by flames; my life is intertwined with them as they dance between the glow of golden yellow and streaks of fiery orange, bringing life to darkness.

My first master was a flame thrower who travelled from fair to fair in northern Italy. At the command of a tinkling bell, I was taught to take a candle and set some torches alight and give them to my master who would juggle them skilfully. The onlookers would reward him with rapturous applause and I would be sent round to collect money in a velvet cap.

My second owner, Master Rizzio, was also a wanderer. He had seen my tricks and had bought me for a handsome sum. Soon we boarded a vessel in Genoa and sailed from the temperate Liguria to the chilly port of Leith in Scotland.

After a few weeks of unemployment and living in cold lodgings in and around Edinburgh, news came that Queen Mary needed a singer to join her trio of minstrels. Master Rizzio secured an audience in the palace. In the presence of the queen he sang a medley of French and Italian songs in his fine bass voice and accompanied himself on the lute. I was welcomed onto the queen's lap, admired and stroked. We were given fine quarters in Holyrood and our lives were transformed. Soon we became favourites in the queen's inner circle.

Master Rizzio was eager to show off his new position in court but, I must say, he never neglected me and always groomed me and gave me tasty morsels, like juicy plums and roasted nuts to eat.

We began to spend evenings in the company of the queen and her maidservants in the small room beside her bed chamber. The conversation was light-hearted and punctuated with sessions of music and card playing. The queen was now pregnant. She liked to cradle me in her arms like her baby-to-be and ruffle the white fur under my chin. I would be allowed to practise my flame trick. At the command of a royal finger and then the sound of a bell, I would clamber up the curtains, candle in paw, and light the sconces to the delight of all. It was a very good life.

One evening in March when we were in our usual good spirits, the door opened. Her Majesty's husband, Henry Stuart, Lord Darnley, and other men entered the room. I jumped from my master's lap and scuttled under the banquet table. I heard a heated conversation. I saw my master's feet as he clung to the skirt of Queen Mary. A dagger was thrust down into his chest. He was dragged across the floor to the bed-chamber beyond. I heard a dull thud as a lifeless body tumbled down the stairs.

The queen was sobbing uncontrollably; her body was shaking. I emerged from my hiding place and was greeted with great emotion. For a long time she held me tight, rocking to and fro. We were as one, united in our shock and sorrow.

That night she smuggled me under the folds of her cloak, and we escaped from the palace. My nomadic life began again. My daily routine changed. There was little merriment now, my new mistress, the queen, kept me close. I was, I think, a precious memento of my master and of happier days.

In time we moved to the safety of Edinburgh castle. The rooms were bleaker and less homely than the palace. Come the summer, hearts lifted with the birth of the baby prince. A period of happy activity replaced the melancholy.

To me it seemed that the queen had forgiven her husband for his part in the murder of my master, for at the news of him falling ill, she left for Glasgow where he had fled, to nurse him back to health. The two returned to the capital, she to Prince James and me in the castle, and he to comfortable lodgings in the old provost's house at Kirk o' Fields.

It was to that house that I was taken on a dark February night, almost a year after the death of my dear Master Rizzio. The company was mostly unfamiliar, a group of men with low secretive voices. I was set on the shoulder of a young

EL GRECO (DOMENIKOS THEOTOKOPOULOS)
An Allegory ('Fábula'), c.1580–5
NG 2491 · Accepted in lieu of tax, with additional funding from the National Heritage Memorial Fund, the Art Fund and Gallery funds 1989

man, and with an older companion at our side.

We crept towards the house carrying two casks of gunpowder. A piece of torch paper was lit to bring a little light into the dark courtyard. The door was forced open and we entered the house. With silent footsteps we made our way to a small room. The three of us huddled round the flame of the torchlight. The faces of my guardians glowed in concentration. The flickering light was magnetic. A small candle was withdrawn from a pouch. With a trembling hand and a gentle puff of breath, the candle flame was kindled. I watched transfixed.

The young man caught my gaze; I was given the candle. He lifted his finger in a familiar command. I suddenly realised

I had a part to play. The sense of anxiety was transmitted to me. I felt scared. I dreaded the sound of the bell. The two men departed. I was alone.

The bell rang. I did not move. I had no audience to play to. No applause. No caresses. Seconds passed. The bell rang again. It was louder this time.

There was a movement above and I heard Lord Darnley's voice as he called to his menservants. The silence was broken. I raised the candle and lit the fuse, which spat crackles as its harsh white flame hissed towards the caskets.

[CATEGORY A]

67

My Last Venice

by JAMES GAO

I do not think my memory does
the square justice – because I take a step back and see nothing.

    there was a storm
      that turned the buildings dark with
rain,

 except, in my memories, the dark bits of that
 storm were white – like they were fading;

the architecture switching between time

lines, unsure towers and
    gothic arches smudge over;
    forgotten. somewhere in the distance
    is a hill, Byzantine I think, the palest I've
    ever cared to remember.

      this shade of red
    is also wrong. bricks were more terracotta
    than this; more sandy to touch. they turn into
mere blueprints of themselves; footprints of people.

for there is no sound in my memory. But, if everything
    else is quiet, I might sometimes hear the whistle
    of a person – a child –, in the bottom
    left corner (their face is pastel impressioned)

or maybe it was a wind: an Italian
    breeze – the calm before a storm. I can see
people running in this memory, but they never move,
always in this perpetual state of having one leg in the air.

their faces look at me; know that it is my fault
    they're peeling like paint, blaming me
with misty-milk eyes that seek solace elsewhere.

    in the background, I think
there's a bronze bell marching, in a dry fashion –

melancholia, for

Italian summers are a parched thing. dust
clouds turn the streets into pointillist paintings,
dots by dots is how I see Venice. dots by dots
I'm making out the details of my hot *piazzetta* and

    why it looks so made up. at the same time
    nothing makes it up, because those cut
    out card board buildings can
    only occupy one dimension.

I sense right through them;
behind those chalky churches are signals and flesh;
neurons mess. you can't see them, but nonetheless…

 I am sure the tour guide said: *there are*
                 no storms in June
                    in Italy
    in broken English. so in one memory or another, I asked him
what that was, pointing towards the pale
burning patch that was the sky. two monoliths,

    hold it up, whilst their marble pencil scratches

    (to the point of it being minimalist),
      dissolve into the background dust. Vanish
    into the rain that washes it all away.

Somewhere deep in this memorymaze

is the flash of hot lightening. Electrical; impulsing
    one corner of this reverie to the next, connecting

objects with a rip, like the rip of white Polaroids
    that captured my lazy sepia season,
or the washed out, blinding flash of a camera. over-exposure.
    cracks in the paper, letting light in;
    I faintly recall being faintly alone in a church,
and opening the door allowed slithers of light
  to pierce these ritualistic shadows,

yet I don't remember thunder. As I said, my memories

are devoid of sound.

        and every other sense is fading, fading away
        like a lost Summer whisper in a silent crowd.

[CATEGORY C]

JOSEPH MALLORD WILLIAM TURNER
*The Piazzetta, Venice, c.*1835
D NG 871 · Henry Vaughan Bequest 1900

69

Ad Nusquam (Creating an Allegory)

by JEAN TAYLOR

First choose your objects
determine their symbolic meanings.
Make sure that you include
some people, or at least a skull.
Take care to layer your textures:
old oak, naturally light-absorbing;
pewter, reflective and unforgiving,
velvet, vellum, glass and leather.

Place them for maximum effect,
exploit both light and shade,
introduce chiaroscuro.
Pervert the sinister.
Instead let the light fall from
the left so that it is the right
that finds itself in shadow.

Introduce a casement window
symbolising Christianity.
Let it pour itself in spangling
rays onto a globe which stands
for this planet or any other planet
you choose to travel to or from.

Beside the globe, remember to place
an open book, precisely illustrated
by a now-blind monk, symbolising
education, artistic merit,
literary wisdom, personal sacrifice.

And then a young man with a violin
held, as it might be, at half-mast.
You can choose to make the violin
an emblem of womanhood played
upon, or let it stand purely for music,
in all its forms.

But perhaps you should denote
it to be the indication of a dilettante.
Order it so that the young man faces
away from the light. In his right hand
place a limp bow and let his left
fondle its fern-fiddle neck.
As this is your allegory, you are
permitted to place your own
interpretation on each piece.

Lay a flagon on the floor. Make it
suggestive of draining, wasting
the water, the wine, life's opportunity.
Set alongside it, an unidentified
object. Art must reserve itself
some mystery, some vestige
of the impenetrable.

Then move yourself into the shadow.
Place, at its edge, a bound book,
encrusted with precious stones,
full of forbidden knowledge.
Leave it unopened. Draw your
conclusion in the deepest shadows.
Build, in the darkness, a flight of stairs,
leading, irresistibly, to nowhere.

[CATEGORY E]

GERRIT DOU
An Interior with a Young Violinist, 1637
NG 2420 · Purchased with the aid of the National
Heritage Memorial Fund 1984

Index